Intimacy By Design
© 2025 **Claire Staton**
All rights reserved.

ISBN: 978-1-960862-04-4

Cover Design & Interior Layout: Designed by Josh Pene
Published by: Claire Staton
Printed in the United States of America

Scripture References: Unless otherwise noted, Scripture quotations are from
the **Holy Bible, New International Version®, NIV®**. Copyright © 1973, 1978,
1984, 2011 by Biblica, Inc. Used by permission. All rights reserved worldwide.

For permissions, inquiries, or more information, visit:
PowerOfJesusInTheEveryDay.com

INTIMACY
BY DESIGN

An invitation for parents and preteens/
teens to explore God's blueprints
together through honest conversations
about the beauty of love and intimacy
as God intentionally designed it.

CLAIRE STATON

Acknowledgments:

To my husband, Jonathan —
Thank you for showing me the beauty of intimacy within the safety and protection of our committed marriage. You are the only person who gets to see every part of me, and you continually love and forgive me with the Spirit's help, just as Jesus does. Through you, I am reminded of the ultimate intimacy we will one day experience fully in heaven.

To the Holy Spirit —
You have been my greatest teacher, patiently reshaping my heart to love God's design for intimacy more than the world's version. Over the past decade, You've led me on a journey to discover that the truest joy is being perfectly seen and fully loved by God. Thank You for opening my eyes to the beauty of His plan and for drawing me closer to His heart every step of the way.

About the Author

I believed the lies early—lies that said love was about being wanted, desired, or chosen based on how I looked or what I gave. I chased the world's version of intimacy: quick affection, shallow approval, and moments that felt like love but left me emptier every time. I gave away pieces of my heart thinking it would make me whole, but all it did was wound me deeper.

For over a decade, I walked through the consequences of believing what culture says about sex, love, and identity. I wrestled with shame, regret, and the aching feeling that I had missed something deeper. But God, in His kindness, didn't leave me there. He gently rewrote my story—not by shaming me into purity (protecting my eyes, ears, heart and body), but by showing me the beauty of His original design: intimacy rooted in commitment, safety, and selfless love. Intimacy that points us to the kind of closeness we were made for—with Him.

This book was born from that journey. It's the book I wish I had as a preteen/teenager—a guide that goes beyond "don't do this" and instead shows the why behind God's wisdom. I don't want another teen to walk blindly into the traps I did, or another parent to feel unequipped to walk with their child through these conversations.

I want young people to know the truth: You are already loved. You don't have to prove your worth with your body. You were made for lasting connection, not temporary attention. And the intimacy God designed is not shameful—it's sacred. It's powerful. And it's worth waiting for.
Let's reclaim the beauty the enemy tried to steal.
With much prayer and love for you,

-Claire Staton

Contents

Getting Started

Growing up isn't just about getting older—it's about seeing yourself and the world around you more clearly. And some things are too important to figure out on your own. Love, relationships, sex, and intimacy weren't meant to be a guessing game. That's why you're here—because your parents see your independence growing and want to walk with you through these topics. Not with a list of rules, but with wisdom that helps you see the bigger picture of what God designed. This isn't about fear or making you feel bad or guilty. It's about clarity, confidence, and discovering how real love—love that reflects God's heart—is so much greater than what the world makes love out to be.

Let's be real—when it comes to love and sex, you've probably heard a lot of different things. Friends joke about it, social media is all about it, and when adults bring it up, it's often awkward or confusing. Maybe you've wondered: *What's actually true? What does this all mean for me? Why should I even care to have my own thoughts on these subjects and especially at my age?* That's what this devotional is here for—not to tell you what you can't do, but to help you understand why these things matter so much. God isn't holding out on you; He's inviting you into something bigger and better—something that leads to lasting joy instead of unnecessary heartache.

God sees sex as something special and joyful—a gift He created for a husband and wife to share in marriage. It's meant to be a safe and loving way for them to come together as one. But it's about more than just marriage! Ephesians 5:31-32 NIV says that the closeness between a husband and wife is like the way Jesus loves the Church—selfless, forgiving, and full of care. Sex is part of that love, showing the trust and intimacy God designed for marriage from the very beginning, for he is the original creator of sex and marriage.

Over fourteen chapters, you'll dive deep into what love truly means, beyond just romance or the feelings we see in movies. You'll explore how real love is about commitment, selflessness, and seeing others the way God does. You'll also learn how sex is more than just a physical act—it's part of God's beautiful design for marriage full of trust, faith, and a lifelong promise between a husband and wife that reflects the ultimate picture of the gospel. But intimacy doesn't start or end with sex. You'll see how emotional and spiritual intimacy are just as important, shaping the way we connect, feel safe, and experience deep, meaningful relationships—not just in marriage, but in friendships and family too. Through these chapters, you'll gain wisdom that will help you see love, relationships, and your own worth through God's eyes, giving you confidence and clarity to navigate these topics with truth and purpose.

HOW TO USE THIS DEVOTIONAL
Creating a Safe and Meaningful Conversation Space

We know that conversations about love, relationships, sex, and intimacy can sometimes feel awkward or difficult. That's why we intentionally designed this devotional to be a **judgment-free space** where both parents and preteens/teens can feel comfortable sharing their thoughts, questions, and experiences. To help guide this, we've included four key elements in each chapter:

1. Overview of God's Heart
This first section is an overview of God's heart—a way to help you start thinking about sex, love, and relationships the way God does, so you can live the joyful, free life He designed for you.

God created love, connection, and even sex to be beautiful, powerful gifts. But the enemy and this world doesn't want you to enjoy those gifts the right way. He wants to confuse you, distract you, and lead you into things that seem exciting for a moment but actually hurt your heart, steal your peace, and leave you feeling empty.

That's why there is so much information out there—on the internet, in songs, in shows—that twists what God made good and tries to keep you trapped in sin, lust and selfishness. The world often tells you love is just about feelings or attraction, and sex is something you can use whenever you want. But that's not what brings lasting joy to your life.

When we follow Jesus, we discover something better:
- A kind of love that truly satisfies us and is not based on what we do or don't do.
- A kind of closeness that is safe, lasting, and full of joy.
- A life that blesses others instead of using them.
- A purpose of pointing people to Jesus that is so fulfilling.

God's design is not about rules to ruin your fun—it's about a loving Father who created YOU and therefore knows you better than anyone in this world and know exactly what YOUR heart really needs to thrive. His way ALWAYS leads to freedom, joy, and connection, and He invites you to walk in it.

2. The Parents' Promise:
A Commitment to Safe, Open Conversations

We created the **Parents' Promise** section to set the tone for honest,
open, and respectful dialogue. These simple commitments help
ensure that your preteen/teen feels safe to share, process, and explore
their thoughts without fear of judgment or overreaction. The promise
statements are listed together in **Appendix A,** so at any time, your
child can refer back to them and gently remind you if they feel the
conversation is straying from a place of safety and respect.
The goal is to **create an atmosphere where listening is just as
important as speaking.** A lot of people need space and silence before
they feel ready to open up, and that's okay. The promises are a way
to hold space for each other so this devotional becomes **a place of
connection, not lecturing.**

Additionally, in **Appendix B,** there is a **blank list of vows** for preteens/
teens to fill out at the end of the devotional. This allows them to create
their own promises for themselves—if they choose—to help them fully
experience the joy and freedom Jesus has for them in this life. Whether
it's a commitment to pursue purity (protecting your heart, ears, eyes
and body), to turn to God when they're struggling, or to be honest with
a trusted adult when facing tough situations, this is their opportunity to
take ownership of their journey with God.

3. Questions:
Fostering Meaningful Two-Way Conversations

The **discussion questions** are crafted to spark real, honest conversations—not just another lecture. These questions are designed to encourage both parents and preteens/teens to share. No one should dominate the discussion; instead, it should be a **mutual exchange**, where both listening and speaking matter.

There will be moments of silence, and that's perfectly fine. Sometimes, giving people space to think allows them to process and express their thoughts in a way that feels natural to them. These questions are here to **invite curiosity, reflection, and deeper connection,** not to force a certain response.

4. Drawing Closer:
Seeing Jesus in Everyday Moments

At the end of each chapter, the **Drawing Closer: Seeing Jesus in Everyday Moments** section is included as a special moment to shift the focus from just knowing about these truths to truly experiencing them. This is my heart behind this devotional—**praying that preteens/teens experience true intimacy with Jesus.**

If they develop a deep, personal connection with Him, these truths won't just be information; they'll transform the way they see love, relationships, and themselves. This section gives them a moment to **invite Jesus into their thoughts and emotions, ask Him to reveal His love, and reflect on how His truth applies to their everyday life.**

One way to use this section is to **separate it from the main devotional time—**perhaps reading a chapter a week and do a midweek connection time to circle back to the Drawing Closer section and see what God has spoken to them.

Whatever works best for your family, the most important thing is to **encourage an ongoing relationship and awareness of Jesus, where they see His power at work in their life.**

INTRODUCTION:
So What Even is Intimacy?

Intimacy is a close, special kind of friendship where you feel safe, known, and loved—just as you are.

And guess what? **God is the one who created it.** He made intimacy because He made us in His image and He loves us and wants us to know what it feels like to be fully known and still fully loved no matter what.

From the very beginning, God made people to be close to Him and to each other. That kind of closeness is meant to show us a little picture of the perfect relationship we'll one day have with Him in heaven, where there's no sin, no shame, no fear, no hurt, and nothing getting in the way of being deeply loved and known by Him.

But even now, God gives us the gift of intimacy here on earth. We can have it in different ways:
- **With God:** talking to Him, worshiping, doing what He made you to love to do and knowing He sees your heart and still loves you completely.
- **With family and friends:** laughing, playing, working together, serving, crying, praying, sharing secrets, or just being together without needing to pretend or perform.
- **In marriage:** a husband and wife are invited into the deepest kind of intimacy—a safe place where two people choose to know and love each other emotionally, spiritually, and physically. Here's what that looks like:
    - **Emotional intimacy** is when you share your feelings and feel safe to be real, even when you're having a hard day.
    - **Spiritual intimacy** is when you grow together in your relationship with God—praying, reading the Bible, and reminding each other of His truth.
    - **Physical intimacy** comes last, like the icing on a cake, and is a way husbands and wives show their love and closeness with their bodies enjoying each other and becoming one. God designed this part only for marriage, to protect it and make it special.

God designed intimacy as a gift—not just to make us happy, but to remind us how deeply He loves us.

When we experience that kind of closeness—with Him and with others—it points our hearts back to the gospel:
- That Jesus saw everything about us—even our sin—and still came near.
- He gave His life on the cross to pay for our mistakes, and then He rose from the dead to make a way for us to be close to God forever.
- Now, anyone who trusts Him can have a forever friendship with God—one where you're never alone, always loved, and fully known.

That's the kind of intimacy (closeness) our hearts were made for. And that's what God specifically designed to give to us.

CHAPTER 1
Marriage as a Picture of the Gospel

Think about your best friend—the one who is always there for you, no matter what. They laugh with you when you're happy, help you when you're sad, and stick with you through all the tough times. Now, imagine they make a promise to always be there for you, even when things are hard. That's what marriage is like, but it's even more powerful because it shows us something deeper: a picture of Jesus' love for us.

In the Bible, marriage is described as a covenant, which is a special promise between two people. But this promise is different from any other—it's a promise to stay committed, to always love, and to always care for each other, no matter what happens. And this covenant is meant to reflect how much Jesus loves us unconditionally. Ephesians 5:31-32 says that when a husband and wife come together as one flesh, their love shows us something even bigger: it's a picture of Jesus and His church (that's God's people). Here's how it works:

The husband is called to love his wife the way Jesus loves the church. That means a husband should be ready to lay down his life for his wife— just like Jesus gave His life for us. Jesus didn't just say He loved us; He showed it by dying for us to save us. A husband's love should be the same kind of sacrificial love, asking the Spirit to continually help him put his wife's needs above his own and serving her with kindness and care.

The wife is called to honor and follow her husband, similar to how the church trusts and follows Jesus. Jesus listens to God and does what God asks. In the same way, the husband is called to listen and follow Jesus and as he does this the wife is called to support her husband, trusting his leadership to lead and guide them. But this doesn't mean being controlled—it's about working together in love, each person supporting the other as they are following God.

This kind of love isn't just about feelings or what's easy—it's about a promise to love and serve each other even at our worst, just like Jesus loves us. It's sacrificial, patient, and ready to forgive.

Inside this marriage covenant, sex is a way for the husband and wife to celebrate their deep love and commitment. It's not just about pleasure or physical closeness—it's a part of their promise to each other, a special way to show they are one. Just like Jesus is one with the church, a husband and wife become one, sharing a love that reflects God's love for them.
Marriage is beautiful because it's not just about two people being in love; it's about pointing the world to Jesus' perfect love. It's a love that's faithful, sacrificial, and persevering. And when you see marriage as a picture of the gospel, you understand that it's more than just a promise between two people—it's a living, breathing example of how much God loves us.

In marriage, the husband and wife both show the love of Jesus: the husband by laying down his life for his wife, and the wife by supporting and honoring her husband, just as we are called to follow Christ. It's a beautiful reminder that true love isn't just about feelings—it's about the commitment to care for, serve, and love each other even when we don't deserve it.

Drawing Closer: *Seeing Jesus in Everyday Moments*

Jesus is the greatest example of love there is—He traded His life for us. Ask God to Show Up: "Lord, let me see Your unstoppable love in my daily life. Reveal moments where Your faithfulness shines, so I can marvel at how You never give up on me."

Practical Note: As you notice God's steady care—maybe in a friend's kindness or timely encouraging word—think about how this reflects the loyalty spouses show each other in marriage.

Parents' Promise

We promise to **listen calmly** as we talk about marriage together and how it reflects the gospel. Let's explore God's design together.

Questions

1. What's one thing you learned today? (This helps our brain remember!)

____

____

____

____

2. Did you know marriage is like a picture of how much Jesus loves us?

____

____

____

____

3. How does that change the way you think about marriage?

____

____

____

____

4. How easy or hard is it to believe God loves you that much? (It's okay
   to be honest!)

____

____

____

____

5. Where do you see God loving you in everyday life? (Like through
   people, things, or moments?)

____

____

____

____

____

____

____

____

____

____

____

____

CHAPTER 2
God's Heart for Deep Connection

God made us to long to feel close to people because He Himself is the most beautiful example of it. In the Bible, we learn that God exists as Father, Son, and Holy Spirit—three persons, but one God. This relationship is perfect, full of love, trust, and unity. The Father, the Son (Jesus), and the Holy Spirit have been living in perfect closeness with each other from the very beginning. They support, love, and work together to fulfill God's plan for the world.

God has always been in perfect relationship—community, and He made us to share in that. When God created us, He gave us a desire to feel like others truly know us and understand us. The Father, Son, and Spirit know everything about each other, and God placed that same longing in us. Only He can fully meet it, but He also designed us to experience glimpses of that closeness with others. He gives us the gift of friendship and family, and—if we choose—an even deeper gift in marriage. Marriage is where someone gets to know you so closely, day by day, in ways no one else does. They see the hidden parts, the little things, the everyday moments—what a privilege. It's not good for us to be alone (Genesis 2:18) because God created us to experience true connection and partnership, just like He does with the Son and the Holy Spirit.

We are stronger together. God made us to have relationships—to love, support, and grow together. That's why God made woman for man. He didn't want Adam to be alone, and He doesn't want us to be alone either. We were made for community—with God, and with each other.

Marriage is one of the most special relationships God made. It's not just about having fun or living in the same house. It's about choosing to love someone every single day, when they're at their best and when they're having a hard time. That kind of love doesn't come from trying really hard. It comes from looking at Jesus. Because Jesus saw all our mistakes, all the times we would ignore Him or mess up, and He still chose to love us. He even died for us while we were still doing wrong. In marriage, we get to remember that kind of love. When we make mistakes, we can say, "God doesn't stop loving me—and I won't stop loving you." And when things are great and full of joy, we celebrate together and thank God for the gift of each other. Marriage is a place where two people help each other grow— not just grow up, but grow kinder, gentler, more forgiving, and more like Jesus. It's not always easy, but it's beautiful, because it's a picture of the kind of love God has for us— a love that never gives up.

Even as a preteen, you can begin to understand that real relationships are about more than just fun or feeling happy. They're about the deep connection God created us to have—a connection where we share our hearts, support each other, and build each other up. Marriage, when it focuses on the love of the Father, Son, and Holy Spirit, shows us the goodness of knowing a lot about someone and how we were made to experience love in the deepest ways, just like God Himself does.

This longing for community is not only a gift, it's God's plan—and it's really good.

Drawing Closer: *Seeing Jesus in Everyday Moments*

Jesus wants a true connection with us, not surface-level faith.
Ask God to show you how He's with you even in simple moments, so you
can sense the real closeness He offers.

Practical Note: Maybe at lunch or before bed, pause to notice a small
moment—a friend's text or a warm meal.

Parents' Promise

We promise to be **curious instead of lecturing.** Your views on genuine
connection and how it relates to Jesus matter, and we'll welcome them
openly.

Questions

1. When was a time you felt close to someone and how did you enjoy it?

____

____

____

2. How can you and God get to know each other more closely?

____

____

____

3. What are some ways married people know each other more than others?

____

____

____

____

4. What would life be like if no one really knew you—not your thoughts, your feelings, or what you're going through?

____

____

____

____

5. Why do you think God gave us the gift of getting to know people closely—like friends, family, or even a husband or wife?

____

____

____

____

____

____

____

____

____

CHAPTER 3

God's Design: Male and Female Reflecting His Image

From the very beginning, God created people to be different but equal. He made male and female on purpose, and together they show a fuller picture of who God is—God the Father, Jesus the Son, and the Holy Spirit. Men often reflect God's strength, leadership, and protection. Women often reflect God's nurturing heart, wisdom, and beauty. Neither is better—they are both needed to show the world what God is like.

But here's something important: not every boy looks or acts the way the world thinks a "man" should. Maybe you're not super into sports, or maybe you care more about art, music, or reading. That doesn't make you less of a man. God made you with your own gifts and passions for a reason. Don't let labels from other people tell you who you are. God already decided who you are—you're His.

The enemy and the world will try to tell you that you can choose something different from what God made you to be. It might sound like freedom, but it actually leads to more loneliness and less peace. God's design isn't meant to hold you back—it's meant to help you thrive, to know who you are, and to live with joy and purpose.

When we understand that our differences as men and women are good and part of God's plan, we stop competing and start working together. That's when friendships, families, and communities grow stronger. We learn to honor and respect each other, seeing the unique ways God has made us to point people to His love. And through it all, people get to see more clearly how big and diverse God's love really is.

Drawing Closer: Seeing Jesus in Everyday Moments

God created male and female in His image to show the world different aspects of His character. Ask God to show you specific differences this week and take time to celebrate the differences instead of comparing or competing."

Parents' Promise

We commit to letting you **explore your thoughts** without judgment.

Questions

1. When you look at how God made boys and girls, what does it show you about Him?

\
\
\

2. How does knowing that God made both male and female on purpose help you see others differently?

\
\
\

3. What are some ways you can show encouragement and respect to others—especially people who are different from you?

____

____

____

____

4. If you were God's enemy and wanted to ruin His good design, how would you try to break or twist it?

____

____

____

____

5. How do you see the world trying to change what God designed?

____

____

____

____

____

____

____

____

____

CHAPTER 4
Celebrating Sex as a Gift in Marriage

Imagine opening a birthday present from someone who really knows you—a gift that makes you feel special, loved, and cared for. That's a little like how sex feels in marriage: a gift that says, "I see you, I trust you, and I'm excited to share this with you." It's not something casual or embarrassing. It's a way for husband and wife to honor and enjoy each other in a safe, loving marriage where they've made a lifelong promise to be there for each other.

It's giving a piece of your heart to someone. Doing it in marriage protects you from the heartache of giving your heart to someone who does not handle it with care or permanence. Sex is the most intimate act you can do with someone because you are connected as one in that moment.

But, just like a birthday gift isn't the only part of a relationship, sex is just one special piece of the bigger picture. Marriage is built on things like being there for each other, listening to each other's feelings, thoughts, and dreams, reminding each other of Jesus' love, and daily kindness that chooses to serve each other.

Like the colors on a painting, sex is one of the vibrant, joyful parts that celebrate two people who are already united in love, saying, "We're in this together!"

As you grow up, it's important to know that sex is a special gift from God. It's not something to be embarrassed about or treated like it doesn't matter. God made it on purpose—to be a way for a husband and wife to enjoy closeness and the deepest love here on Earth. When you understand that it's meant for marriage, you begin to see your body and heart as something extremely valuable— a gift that only one special person, your future spouse, will have the honor to know completely.

Marriage is a promise to love each other for life. And in that safe, committed love, you give every part of yourself— not just your body, but your heart, your dreams, your fears, your whole self. Someone who hasn't promised to love you for life doesn't get the gift of knowing every part of you. That kind of love is meant to be protected— and saved for someone who sees you as a treasure and chooses every part of you for life.

That is the kind of intimacy (closeness) that respects each other's hearts and embodies the way God designed it to be a gift for our good.

Drawing Closer: *Seeing Jesus in Everyday Moments*

Jesus fills our days with gifts we don't earn—starting with salvation. When we notice and thank Him for the small blessings, we train our hearts to see His goodness everywhere.

Practical Note: Next time someone shares a kind word, gives you a hug, or offers you a snack, whisper a quick prayer: "Thank You, Jesus, for showing me Your love in this." Learning to see everyday gifts helps us treasure the bigger ones, like intimacy in marriage, as God intended.

Parents' Promise

We promise to stay **open-minded** when talking about the joy and celebration of sex within marriage. We value your curiosity, no matter how big or small your questions.

Questions

1. What do you think about sex being a gift from God?

2. What are some things the world says about sex, and how are those messages different from what God says?

3. How can we protect the gift of sex?

____

____

____

____

4. Why do you think only our husband or wife should have the gift of
   knowing all of us—our body, heart, and soul?

____

____

____

____

5. What does respecting your body and heart look like?

____

____

____

____

____

____

____

____

____

____

____

____

CHAPTER 5
What Really Matters in a Relationship

You might see people on TV or in videos who like each other just because they look good. But in real life, what really matters is who a person is on the inside.

Someone's character and heart is how they treat people—are they kind? Honest? Do they receive God's love and help others? Do you see the fruit of the Spirit (joy, peace, kindness, self control, etc)? Those are the things that make someone great to be around, not just their body or style. Looks change and fade, but a heart that loves Jesus gets even more attractive over time.

Imagine having a friend or one day a husband or wife who really understands you—who listens when you're sad, cheers you on when you're trying something new, prays with you, and reminds you that Jesus loves you. That's the kind of love that stays strong.

Marriage isn't about how someone looks or even about kissing or holding hands first. It's about being best friends, trusting each other, and following Jesus together. Then the physical part (like sex) is like a celebration of all that love and closeness you've already built.

Right now, it's good to practice being a good friend—telling the truth, being kind, listening well, and loving others like Jesus does. Those are the things that help you build strong, healthy relationships when you're older.

So don't just look for someone who's cool or popular or gives you butterflies. Look for someone whose heart shines for Jesus—and ask God to help your heart shine too.

What really matters
is who a person is
on the inside.

Drawing Closer: Seeing Jesus in Everyday Moments

Jesus cares deeply about hearts. He wants us to experience closeness that inspires and grows us, rooted in His love.

Practical Note: Think of one person you can be real with this week. Share something honest—maybe a prayer request or what God's teaching you. Notice how true closeness grows when love and faith are shared.

Parents' Promise

We promise to **listen closely** to your thoughts about character, friendship, and what matters most. We value your perspective and believe God is shaping something beautiful in you.

Questions

1. Which friendships do you have (or want to build) that feel deep and real—not just surface level?

2. What makes someone a really good friend to have?

3. Have you ever had a friend who showed good character, even if they weren't the most popular or fun? What was that like?

____

____

____

____

4. What do you think makes a marriage strong?

____

____

____

____

5. What do you think is the most important part of marriage?

____

____

____

____

____

____

____

____

____

____

CHAPTER 6
Distinguishing Lust from Genuine Love

Lust is like a quick burst of energy—a rush that's focused on getting what you want right now, without thinking about the other person. It's about selfish desires and doesn't last long. On the other hand, genuine love is like a steady campfire—it offers warmth, light, and comfort that lasts over time. Love is about giving, caring, and helping the other person know their worth as God's child. It's patient and kind, while lust is more about getting what you want without considering what's best for the other person.

In marriage, sex is a beautiful expression of genuine love. It grows from a foundation of respect, commitment, and understanding. But lust is different—it reduces a person to an object, focusing only on their body and what they can give. You'll start to notice when someone is focused only on their own desires and doesn't care about your boundaries or feelings. That's when you know they're not honoring the whole you—your mind, heart, and soul—they're only trying to fulfill their own wants.

Understanding the difference between lust and love helps protect you from relationships where you might feel used. When you see love as being patient, kind, and willing to serve the other person, you'll be able to spot when someone is pretending to care, but is actually after their own selfish desires. Knowing what real love looks like helps you stay on a path of healthy, meaningful relationships, keeping you safe from heartbreak and false closeness.

Drawing Closer: *Seeing Jesus in Everyday Moments*

Jesus never used people—He gave His life for them. His love is humble and giving, not selfish.

Practical Note: Ask Jesus this week to help you notice one act of real love and one act of selfishness. When you see His kind of love, pause and say, "Thank You, Jesus, for showing me what love really is."

25

Parents' Promise

We promise to treat your insights on lust and genuine love **with respect**. We're here to help you recognize when someone isn't treating you with the honor you deserve.

Questions

1. When have you felt real love from a friend or family member? What made it feel real?

____

____

____

____

2. Why does lust leave people feeling empty or even hurt?

____

____

____

____

3. What are some ways God shows you His love that never changes and always loves you no matter what?

____

____

____

____

4. Can you tell when someone is being kind because they really care—not just to get something from you?

____

____

____

____

5. Why is it important that someone likes your whole self—not just what's on the outside?

____

____

____

____

____

____

____

____

____

____

CHAPTER 7
Curiosity—A Normal Part of Growing Up

As you grow up, it's totally normal for your mind to be full of questions about crushes, attraction, and how much you should kiss or touch. Curiosity is a sign that you're learning about yourself and the world around you. The big question is: will you ask the right people—like your parents or trusted adults—for answers, or will you let your curiosity lead you into confusing or risky situations?

Talking to your parents about these things might feel awkward at first, but it's kind of like asking a pro chef for the recipe instead of trying to make a meal with random ingredients or learn from someone who has no idea or the wrong recipe entirely. Your trusted adult can give you clear, honest answers about how our bodies work, why sex is meant for marriage, and how you can tell when you're emotionally ready for a relationship. This open conversation helps protect you from the false information that might come from friends or random internet searches.

When you embrace your curiosity in a responsible way, you don't have to treat sex like a secret or feel guilty about it. Instead, you'll see it as a beautiful gift for marriage that you can understand and feel confident in. Learning about it with the guidance of trusted adults helps you make wise decisions and God's truth will protect you from the lies of the world and the deception of the enemy that wants to steal the goodness of God's design for intimacy from you.

Curiosity is a sign you're learning about yourself and the world around you.

Drawing Closer: *Seeing Jesus in Everyday Moments*

Jesus never turned away people who were honestly searching. He welcomed their questions and gave them truth with love.

Practical Note: This week, if you have a question about sex, relationships, or anything that confuses you, whisper a prayer: "Jesus, help me see what's true." Then share your question with a parent or mentor you trust.

Parents' Promise

We promise to honor your questions as important, without jumping to conclusions. We'd rather you ask us than rely on misleading sources.

Questions

1. What kinds of questions do you find yourself most curious about regarding kissing, sex or relationships?

____

____

____

____

2. Why might it be safer to seek answers from parents or mentors than random online content or even friends?

____

____

____

____

3. How might the world or the enemy try to use your curiosity to steal
    God's best from you?

____

____

____

____

4. How can your guardian/parent be someone you feel comfortable
    coming to with questions, even the awkward ones?

____

____

____

____

5. Want to make up a silly code word for when you want to talk about
    something personal but don't want to say it out loud right away?

____

____

____

____

____

____

____

____

____

____

CHAPTER 8
The Gift of Desire and the Wisdom of Timing

Our bodies were designed by God. That includes our feelings, emotions, and even our desires. God created us as whole beings, and He didn't make us to just function—He made us to feel, to experience pleasure, and to enjoy life. That's why He gave us nerve endings all throughout our body and designed sex to be not just about making children, but also about deep connection, intimacy, and yes, even enjoyment. He could have made it just a necessary function, like breathing, but instead, in His kindness, He made it something delightful—because He loves us and wants marriage to be a place of delight, trust, and closeness.

But here's the thing: Just because something is good doesn't mean it's meant for any time or any place. God set up boundaries around intimacy not to take away joy, but to protect it. Think about a bonfire. A fire inside a fireplace is warm, comforting, and safe. It brings people together. But a fire outside the fireplace, in the middle of the living room floor? That same fire now becomes destructive. It can spread quickly and cause harm. The fire itself isn't bad—it just needs to be in the right place at the right time.

That's why God warns us about awakening these desires too soon (Song of Solomon 8:4 NIV). Masturbation (touching ourselves) is one of those things that can feel private, harmless, and even natural—but when we engage in it outside of marriage, we're awakening a fire that isn't yet meant to burn. It's similar to sex in the way it stirs up feelings and desires, but without the covenant and safety of marriage to protect it. And here's where wisdom comes in: once you start something like this, it often doesn't stop there. It can lead to wanting more and more—more stimulation, more curiosity, more things to satisfy desires that weren't meant to be satisfied outside of marriage. What starts as a habit can quickly become a struggle, leading to guilt, secrecy, and even addiction.

God isn't out to shame you for your feelings—He made you with them. But He also gave you wisdom, self-control, and His Spirit to guide you. His design for intimacy is so much greater than momentary pleasure. It's about something lasting, something whole.

If you've already struggled with this, know that God's grace covers you, and it's never too late to bring it to Him and ask for His help and a trusted adult. He isn't disappointed in you—He's inviting you into something better. And if you haven't struggled with it yet, consider this your reminder to guard your heart and body with wisdom. When the time is right, in the safety and joy of marriage, these desires will be fully celebrated. Until then, trust that God's design and timing are always the best for you.

Drawing Closer: Seeing Jesus in Everyday Moments

Jesus loves when you talk to Him. You don't need fancy words—just be honest. Tell Him how you're feeling about this topic and ask Him to fill your heart so you don't have to chase love in the wrong places.

Practical Note: Look for His closeness today in small things: a smile, a peaceful moment, or just knowing He's listening.

Parents' Promise

We promise to approach this conversation with honesty and understanding, without shame or embarrassment, so you feel safe asking questions and sharing your thoughts.

Questions

1. Have you ever wanted something right away, but later realized waiting was actually better?

____

____

____

____

2. Why do you think God gives us feelings and desires instead of making us like robots?

____

____

____

____

3. Have you ever felt curious about touching yourself or wondering about sex?

____

____

____

____

4. What can you do when you feel tempted or curious in private? Who can help you?

____

____

____

____

5. Why do you think sex outside of marriage can be hurtful, even though it's something God made to be good?

____

____

____

____

____

____

____

____

____

____

CHAPTER 9
The Danger of Pornography & The Call to Purity

God made every part of you to honor Him. Purity means keeping each part focused on what's good, true, and loving so you can stay close to Jesus.

- **Your Eyes:** Purity means paying attention to what you look at. If a show, video, or picture makes you feel weird inside or pulls your thoughts away from God, that's the Holy Spirit nudging you. You can choose to look away and fill your eyes with things that remind you of God's goodness—like nature, art, or people being kind.

- **Your Ears:** Purity means noticing what you listen to. Some music or jokes sound fun but secretly plant lies about love, bodies, or who you are. Instead, choose words, songs, and conversations that build you up and make you feel closer to Jesus.

- **Your Heart:** Purity means letting your heart be full of Jesus' love so you don't feel like you need attention or approval to matter. When you feel lonely, jealous, or like you're "not enough," tell Jesus. He wants to be the One who fills your heart first.

- **Your Mind:** Purity means guiding your thoughts. When your mind wanders to things you know aren't good—or when you replay mean words or scary ideas—you can stop and pray, "Jesus, help me think about what's true." He'll help you replace the lies with His truth.

- **Your Body:** Purity means using your body to honor God. That might look like wearing clothes that don't try to get attention but show you love the body God gave you. It also looks like saving private touches and romantic closeness for marriage, and instead using your body now to give hugs, help others, and serve with joy.

Purity isn't just about *not doing* something. It's about saying *yes* to God's best for you—choosing love, truth, and joy over what might feel good for a moment but hurt later.

One way the enemy wants to trade your purity for lesser things is through pornography. Pornography is pictures, videos, or words that show people's private body parts or sexual acts outside of marriage. It tries to turn something God made to be special and holy—sex between a husband and wife—into entertainment. It is one of the biggest lies the world tells about love and intimacy. It makes people seem like objects instead of precious children of God. It tricks our minds into thinking that love is only about physical things, when real love is about trust, kindness, and respect.

The truth is, porn is addictive. It pulls people in and makes it hard for them to see others the way God does. It can also change the way you think about relationships into unhealthy ways. But you don't have to fall into that trap! God wants you to fill your heart and mind with things that bring life and joy, not things that lead to shame and emptiness.

If you've ever seen pornography, don't keep it a secret. Talk to someone you trust—a parent, a mentor, or a pastor. When you bring things into the light, shame loses its power. God's love is always bigger than any mistake, and He offers you a fresh start every day. Choose to set your eyes and mind on things that are healthy for you, and you'll experience real freedom and joy.

Drawing Closer: Seeing Jesus in Everyday Moments

Jesus wants your heart and mind to be filled with things that bring you closer to Him, not things that leave you empty. His love gives real peace that lasts.

Practical Note: The next time you feel sad, stressed, or bored, notice what you reach for first—a screen, a snack, or something else. Before you do that, pause and whisper, "Jesus, I need You." Read a verse or pray. See if His peace feels different than the quick fix.

Parents' Promise

We promise to create a safe, open space for you to talk about tough topics, help you guard your heart, and guide you in choosing purity and God's truth over harmful influences.

Questions

1. Why do you think God wants us to protect our hearts and minds from harmful images and messages?

____

____

____

____

2. What are some things the world says are okay to watch, listen to, or do—but don't really bring joy, respect, or kindness?

____

____

____

____

3. What should you do if you see something that makes you feel weird, uncomfortable, or confused?

____

____

____

____

4. What are some real ways you can choose to stay pure in your thoughts and actions every day?

____

____

____

____

5. How do you think purity helps you stay close to God and feel peace inside?

____

____

____

____

____

____

____

____

____

____

CHAPTER 10
Handling Mistakes with Grace

Mistakes happen to everyone—whether it's crossing a boundary you regret, seeing something you shouldn't, or telling a lie. When guilt hits, it's easy to feel stuck, but remember: God's grace (getting the good you don't deserve) and mercy (not getting the bad you do deserve) is bigger than any mistake you could make. When we feel conviction from the Holy Spirit it is God's kindness that says, that was not right, I still love you and have better for you. And that is a blessing. The enemy will instead try to shame you and tell you how bad you are and attack who you are as a person. Do not listen to that voice. Listen to God's voice that calls you closer to Him with truth and love.

You do not have to live with shame like the enemy wants you to believe, because Jesus already took all of our mistakes on Himself when He died on the cross, offering us forgiveness and a fresh start. That doesn't mean there won't be consequences, but it does mean you don't have to stay trapped in shame. God loves you, and through His grace, He gives you a way to grow stronger and move forward.

The enemy, the devil, wants to make you feel alone, especially when you've made a mistake. He wants you to think that nobody will understand or care so you should hide what's going on inside. He'll even try to pull you away from your parents or trusted adults because he knows secrets will hurt you. But God's truth will set you free. When you bring your struggles into the light and talk about them with people who love you, shame loses its power. God's love and forgiveness are always bigger than our mistakes, and He wants you to come to Him.

Talking to your parents might feel hard, but they love you and want the best for you. They might set boundaries or talk with you about the consequences of your choices, but that's all part of their love and God's protection. God's plan and boundaries aren't meant to restrict you—they're meant to give you the best life. His design for sex and relationships is beautiful and leads to true joy when we follow His path. When you trust God's truth, you can be free from the lies and shame the enemy tries to use to trap you. Your mistakes don't define you; God's love and forgiveness do. And with His grace, you'll grow stronger, closer to Him, and live the life He has always wanted for you.

Drawing Closer: *Seeing Jesus in Everyday Moments*

Jesus never runs out of forgiveness. No matter what you've done, you can turn to Him and be fully forgiven.

Practical Note: When you feel weighed down by guilt, stop and pray: "Jesus, please forgive me." Then pay attention to how He comforts you— maybe through Scripture, a parent's encouragement, or a sense of peace in your heart.

Parents' Promise

We promise to offer grace and guidance when mistakes happen. You won't lose our love; we'll work together to learn and grow from these experiences.

Questions

1. Have you ever done something wrong and felt like hiding? What did that feel like?

2. What's the difference between feeling bad because you messed up and feeling like you're a bad person?

3. Why do you think the enemy wants you to keep secrets and feel alone?

____

____

____

____

4. What do you think Jesus wants you to do after you make a mistake?

____

____

____

____

5. Who are safe people you can talk to when you feel stuck or ashamed?

____

____

____

____

____

____

____

____

____

____

____

CHAPTER 11
Anchoring Your Identity in God's Love

It's easy to think your worth comes from who likes you, what people say about you, or what experiences you've had, but your true worth is unchangeable and given to you only by God your Father and Creator. People might try to make you feel valuable, or sometimes they might even try to take that worth away, but no person can give or take away your worth because it was never theirs to give or take. You were made by God, and that's where your worth comes from. His love for you is what makes you worth it, and that love will never change.

Your worth cannot be changed based on the approval of others, how many cool things you have, or on how many romantic relationships you have. Sometimes it might feel like you need someone else to make you feel special, but no matter how hard they try, their words and actions will never be enough to fill that deep longing. The truth is, they can't give you the worth that only comes from your Creator. God knows you better than anyone else—He sees every part of you, from every hair on your head to every tear you've cried. He created you for a very specific purpose, and you are His child. Your worth is so deep that God proved it by sending His Son, Jesus, to die for YOU.

No one else can offer that kind of love. God's love for you never changes no matter how much good you do or how many times you mess up. It's not based on what you do or how others look at you. He delights in you because He made you exactly the way you are. God says you are worthy, you matter and you are special, and that truth is written in stone—forever. You are enough just as you are, not because of anything you've done, but because of the way God sees you. He calls you worthy, and His love is what gives you true, lasting value.

When you know you're loved unconditionally by God, you'll see that you have the strength and knowledge from the Spirit to love yourself and others well. You won't let anyone treat you like an object or make you feel less than who you are as God's chosen warrior.

You'll dress with care, carry yourself with kindness and understanding for yourself and others, and be clear about the boundaries you set for how others can treat you. Your identity is grounded in God's love, and that means you won't settle for anything less than the love, care, and respect that you deserve. You'll approach every relationship knowing that your worth and your friends/family's worth are both priceless and no one needs to prove their worth to anyone—because God already has.

Drawing Closer: *Seeing Jesus in Everyday Moments*

Jesus doesn't wait for you to be perfect—He meets you in your struggles and calls you valuable. His love proves your worth.

Practical Note: When you start to wonder if you're good enough, pause and say: "Jesus, thank You that I'm already loved by You." Let that truth quiet the need for anyone else's approval.

45

Parents' Promise

We promise to continually affirm your worth in God's eyes. We're here to remind you that love isn't earned by meeting romantic or physical expectations—it's already yours.

Questions

1. Who decides how valuable you are—people or God? Why?

____

____

____

____

2. Who are you? What is your identity in God?

____

____

____

____

3. What happens when you try to feel special based on what others
    think of you?

____

____

____

____

4. What do you think it means that God made you and says you are
    special?

____

____

____

____

5. How should you treat yourself and others if God says we are all
    valuable?

____

____

____

____

____

____

____

____

____

____

CHAPTER 12
Setting Boundaries for a Healthy Future

God created intimacy—including sex—as a beautiful gift for marriage. But protecting that gift isn't only about waiting until you're married. It's also about guarding what goes into your heart and mind right now. Think of boundaries like fences around a garden. Fences don't keep the good things out—they help the good things grow strong and healthy by keeping harmful things away. Your heart is like that garden. The shows you watch, the music you listen to, the TikToks or YouTube videos you click on, even the jokes you laugh at—those things are like seeds being planted in your garden. Some will grow into good fruit, helping you be loved by Jesus and love others more. Others can grow into weeds that choke out your joy and blind you to the good things God wants to show you.

When we fill our hearts and minds with things of this world, it's harder to hear God's voice. But when we guard our hearts and focus on what is good, we stay close to Him and hear Him more clearly. Boundaries help keep us from being distracted by lies, so we can enjoy the truth of God's love every single day.

Setting boundaries might mean things like:
- Choosing not to watch shows or videos that make sex, bodies, or relationships seem casual or disrespectful.
- Limiting time alone with friends when it might tempt you to cross lines.
- Deciding not to follow influencers or accounts that make you feel "less than" or lead your thoughts away from God.
- Asking a parent or mentor for help when you see something online that makes you feel weird, guilty, or confused.

These aren't rules meant to take away your fun—they're meant to protect your heart and help you grow in peace, joy, and freedom. Boundaries give you confidence because you already know where the lines are. You don't have to live in constant worry about crossing them. When you understand the "why" behind boundaries, it gets easier to say no to things that look fun but could hurt you in the long run. Instead, you can enjoy the freedom of a heart that's safe, healthy, and filled with good fruit.

And here's the best news: Jesus doesn't love you because you always keep the right boundaries. He already proved His love by dying for you while you were still a sinner (Romans 5:8 NIV). Even when you mess up, His grace is bigger. Because of the gospel—His life, death, and resurrection—you don't have to stay stuck in guilt. You can run back to Him, be forgiven, and start fresh. That's why boundaries aren't about earning God's love—they're about enjoying it more fully and living in the freedom He already gave you.

Drawing Closer: *Seeing Jesus in Everyday Moments*

Jesus also set boundaries, withdrawing to pray and avoiding empty controversies, showing us boundaries can be spiritually healthy. Ask God to Show Up: "Lord, let me see Your power in the boundaries I set. Show me how they protect my heart, just as You protected Your time with the Father, so I can sense peace and focus on what matters."

Practical Note: Identify one boundary you'd like to establish—like screen-time rules or friend-group limits—and ask God to give you peace and clarity as you live it out.

Parents' Promise

We promise to collaborate on boundaries in a respectful way, explaining our reasoning and hearing your input so that you see them as supportive, not stifling.

Questions

1. Why do you think boundaries are actually helpful, not just rules?

____

____

____

____

2. How can your parents or other adults help you make good boundaries?

____

____

____

____

3. Can you think of a time when a boundary helped you stay safe or make a good choice?

____

____

____

____

4. What kinds of things (like shows, jokes, or situations) might pull your heart away from God's good plan?

____

____

____

____

5. How can setting boundaries now help your future marriage and relationships be strong and full of love?

____

____

____

____

____

____

____

____

____

____

CHAPTER 13:
Moving Forward with Joy & Confidence

Jesus loves you. He's not waiting for you to be perfect. He already knows everything about you—when you do good and even when you mess up—and He still chose to die for you so you could be forgiven, free, and close to God forever.

When Jesus came back to life, He crushed the power of sin, fear, and shame. That means no mistake is too big for Him to forgive. You don't ever have to stay stuck in shame. You can run straight to Him, tell Him everything, and know He'll help you grow stronger.

And He didn't leave you to figure it all out alone. Jesus gave you His Spirit to help you live with wisdom—knowing what's true and right and having the courage to do it, even when it's hard.

But there's an enemy who will try to twist God's good truth into lies. Here are some lies you might hear—and the truth from God's Word that sets you free:

1. Identity

- ❖ ***Lie:*** You have to be popular, funny, talented, athletic, or pretty to matter.
- ❖ ***Truth:*** "Before I formed you in the womb I knew you." – Jeremiah 1:5 NIV. God made you on purpose. You don't have to earn His love—He already loves you fully. You are His child, and nothing can change that.

2. Intimacy by Design

- ❖ ***Lie:*** Sex is just something people do when they really like each other.
- ❖ ***Truth:*** "Therefore a man shall leave his father and his mother and hold fast to his wife, and they shall become one flesh." – Genesis 2:24 NIV. God created sex for marriage—a forever promise. It's not just about bodies but about love, trust, safety, and being deeply known.

3. Lust vs. Love

- ❖ ***Lie:*** Love is doing whatever feels good.
- ❖ ***Truth:*** "Love is patient, love is kind… It does not insist on its own way." – 1 Corinthians 13:4-5 NIV. Real love isn't selfish or rushing. Jesus showed real love by laying down his life for us.

4. Boundaries

- ❖ ***Lie:*** If it feels good, do it. Rules don't matter.
- ❖ ***Truth:*** "Above all else, guard your heart, for everything you do flows from it." – Proverbs 4:23 NIV. God gives us boundaries to protect us and help us live free, not weighed down by regret.

5. Purity

- ❖ ***Lie:*** Watching something once won't hurt. Everyone does it.
- ❖ ***Truth:*** "Blessed are the pure in heart, for they will see God." – Matthew 5:8 NIV. What you watch and think about shapes your heart. Purity means saying yes to closeness with God.

6. Shame vs. Grace

- ❖ ***Lie:*** You messed up. You're bad. God's mad at you.
- ❖ ***Truth:*** "There is now no condemnation for those who are in Christ Jesus." – Romans 8:1 NIV. When you mess up, God doesn't push you away. He pulls you close, forgives you, and gives you a fresh start every time.

7. Worth

- ❖ ***Lie:*** You need someone else to choose you to be valuable.
- ❖ ***Truth:*** "See what great love the Father has lavished on us, that we should be called children of God! And that is what we are!" – 1 John 3:1 NIV. You are already chosen, already loved, already treasured by God.

You Were Made for More
God made you on purpose, because He loves you and wants to be close
to you. That's the biggest truth to hold onto.
You were made to:

- **Be loved by God and love Him back**
  You can talk to Him anytime—He's like the best friend who always
  listens.

- **Enjoy Him and the good things He made**
  Sunsets, laughter, music, hugs, puppies, and even yummy food—
  these are gifts from Him for you to enjoy with a thankful heart.

- **Love like Jesus**
  Show kindness, forgive quickly, listen well, and help others feel safe
  and seen—just like Jesus did.

- **Be wise and strong**
  Wisdom means knowing what's right and choosing to do it. God
  gives you strength when it's hard.

- **Respect your body and others**
  Your body is a gift from God, and so is everyone else's. That's why
  we dress in a way that doesn't convey a need to show off our
  beauty for approval or attention of others but to be kept veiled for
  our future spouse as a gift of becoming one.

- **Enjoy deep friendships**
  God made you for connection. Good friends help you follow Jesus,
  and you can be that kind of friend too.

- **Walk in truth and joy—not shame**
  When you mess up, you don't have to hide. Jesus says, "Come to
  Me. I love you, and I'll help you."

*Never forget: You are incredibly valuable—not because of what you do
or what others think—but because God made you, loves you, and sent
Jesus to rescue you. That's the power of the gospel. Nothing can take
that away.*

Drawing Closer: Seeing Jesus in Everyday Moments

Because of Jesus' love, you don't have to fear making the wrong choice. He promises to guide you.

Practical Note: Before saying yes to something you're unsure about, pause and pray: "Lord, is this Your way?" Then look for His answer through Scripture, peace in your heart, or wisdom from a godly mentor.

Parents' Promise

We promise to stay approachable and celebrate God's design for sex and marriage with you. We're here to keep these discussions ongoing, guiding and supporting you without judgment.

Questions

1. Which chapter or idea do you feel most excited to keep in mind as you get older?

2. What do you want to learn more about still?

3. What surprised you or stuck with you the most?

____

____

____

____

4. In what ways have you noticed the enemy trying to convince you to
    believe something that goes against God's truth?

____

____

____

____

5. How has your view of God changed?

____

____

____

____

____

____

____

____

____

____

CHAPTER 14:
The Power of Jesus in the Everyday

Sometimes it's easy to think Jesus only shows up at church, when we pray, or when we read the Bible. But the truth is—Jesus is with you all the time. In the normal, everyday moments of your life. And He doesn't just sit with you—He helps you, teaches you, and changes your heart so you can live the kind of life that's full of joy, peace, and purpose.

When I was younger, I didn't always know that. I believed some lies—like I had to be enough or a certain way for people to love me. I thought if someone liked me, it meant I was special. So I gave my heart away in little pieces, hoping it would make me feel whole. But it didn't. It always left me empty.

It was *Jesus* who showed me the truth. Not just one time at church. But in lots of everyday moments.

- Like when I was lonely and thought I needed someone to make me feel important—He whispered, "You already are. I made you."
- When I felt shame from things I did wrong—He reminded me He had already paid for all of it on the cross, and I could come close again.
- When I wanted to fit in and go along with what others were doing— He gave me the courage to say no and choose something better.

Jesus didn't just save me *once*—He keeps saving me. Every day. From lies. From fear. From trying to earn love. From things that steal peace. And He'll do the same for *you*.

Here's how Jesus might show up in YOUR everyday too if you are listening:

- When you feel left out, Jesus says, "I never leave you."
- When someone is mean, He gives you strength to forgive and not carry that meanness in your heart.
- When you're tempted to look at something online you know isn't right, He helps you turn away and set your eyes on what is good.
- When you're mad at your sibling or feel like yelling, He reminds you to stop and breathe and ask for patience.
- When you feel like you'll never be good enough, He says, "I made you. I chose you. I love you as you are."

The gospel isn't just learned at the beginning of your relationship with Jesus and then moved passed—it's *good news for every moment of every day.* It means you don't have to carry shame. You don't have to earn love. You don't have to pretend you've got it all together. Jesus already knows everything about you—and still says, "You are mine."
His death on the cross wasn't the end of the story. He came back to life—to give *you* new life, an abundant life, right now. Not just someday in heaven, but here, today. He puts His Spirit inside you to help you make wise choices, say no to sin, and yes to love.

So when you're walking through your day, remember:

- Jesus is with you at school, at home, on the playground, soccer field, in the car, and even when you're brushing your teeth.
- You can talk to Him about anything.
- He understands your feelings.
- He gives you the strength to do what's right—even when it's hard.
- No matter what anyone else does or doesn't do – it changes nothing about you. You are still God's Chosen warrior.

You don't need to wait until you're older to live for Jesus. He's already calling you now.

That's the power of Jesus in the everyday.
He changes everything—*starting right where you are.*

Some Encouraging Reminders for You Throughout Your Day:

When You Wake Up
- You feel grumpy and don't want to get out of bed.
    - Jesus gives you strength to start the day and reminds you, "My mercy is new this morning!" (Lamentations 3:23 NIV)

When You're Looking in the Mirror
- You feel like your hair looks weird or your clothes don't look cool.
    - Jesus says, "I made you on purpose, and I don't make mistakes." (Psalm 139:14 NIV)

At School
- You don't understand a math problem and feel like giving up.
    - Jesus helps you stay calm and try again. He says, "I'll give you wisdom." (James 1:5 NIV)
- Someone makes fun of you.
    - Jesus helps you forgive and says, "I was hurt too—but I still loved." (Luke 23:34 NIV)
- You're tempted to laugh at someone else so you'll fit in.
    - Jesus reminds you to be kind even when others aren't. That's real strength.

When You're Alone
- You're bored and tempted to look at something online you shouldn't.
    - Jesus reminds you: "Not everything that looks good is good. I have something better." (1 Corinthians 10:13 NIV)
- You feel curious or confused about sex or relationships.
    - Jesus invites you to ask a parent, not hide in shame. He gives you truth to protect you and give you the best.
- You remember a mistake you made and feel bad.
    - Jesus says, "I already paid for that on the cross. You're forgiven." (1 John 1:9 NIV)

At Lunch
- You're sitting alone, or you feel like no one gets you.
    - Jesus sits with you. He knows how it feels to be left out. He says, "I'm your friend." (John 15:15 NIV)

When Choosing What to Wear
- You want to wear something that gets attention but feels a little off.
    - Jesus reminds you: "You're already chosen. You don't need to show off to be seen." (Colossians 3:12 NIV)

When You're Angry
- Your little sibling ruins your game or takes your stuff.
    - Jesus helps you pause, take a breath, and say something kind. For people are not the enemy.

When You're Talking to Friends
- A friend starts talking about someone else and it doesn't feel right.
    - Jesus helps you change the subject or say, "Let's not talk about them like that."
- Someone tells a dirty joke.
    - Jesus helps you walk away or say, "That's not funny to me." That takes real courage—and He's proud of you.

When You're Thinking
- A thought comes into your mind that doesn't feel right or makes you feel yucky.
    - Jesus helps you take that thought and throw it away. He gives you better ones. (Philippians 4:8 NIV)

At Bedtime
- You feel scared, lonely, or unsure about something.
    - Jesus stays with you. He never sleeps and never leaves. You can talk to Him about anything. (Psalm 4:8 NIV)

Appendix A

We promise to listen calmly as we talk about marriage together and how it reflects the gospel. Let's explore God's design together.

We promise to be curious instead of lecturing. Your views on genuine connection and how it relates to Jesus matter to us, and we'll welcome them openly.

We promise to let you explore your thoughts without judgment. Your perspective matters, and we want this to be a safe place for honest discussions.

We promise to stay open-minded when talking about the joy and celebration of sex within marriage. We value your curiosity, no matter how big or small your questions.

We promise to listen deeply to your thoughts on spiritual and emotional bonds, not focusing solely on physical matters. We value your perspective on healthy, well-rounded intimacy.

We promise to treat your insights on lust and genuine love with respect. We're here to help you recognize when someone isn't treating you with the honor you deserve.

We promise to honor your questions as important, without jumping to negative conclusions. We'd rather you ask us than rely on misleading sources.

We promise to approach this conversation with honesty and understanding, without shame or embarrassment, so you feel safe asking questions and sharing your thoughts.

We promise to create a safe, open space for you to talk about tough topics, help you guard your heart, and guide you in choosing purity and God's truth over harmful influences.

We promise to offer grace and guidance when mistakes happen. You won't lose our love; we'll work together to learn and grow from these experiences.

We promise to continually affirm your worth in God's eyes. We're here to remind you that love isn't earned by meeting romantic or physical expectations—it's already yours.

We promise to collaborate on boundaries in a respectful way, explaining our reasoning and hearing your input so that you see them as supportive, not stifling.

We promise to stay approachable and celebrate God's design for sex and marriage with you. We're here to keep these discussions ongoing, guiding and supporting you without judgment.

Parent Signature ____

Darkness loves secrets. God loves the light.

When you open up to your parents, you slam the door on the enemy's lies and step into God's freedom.

Appendix B – Space for Preteens/Teens' Personal Promises

After everything you've read, if you feel inspired to write personal promises for yourself—commitments that will help you build a strong and thriving life? Use this space to reflect and set intentions for the path ahead.